The Lady of the Fountain

The Lady of the Fountain

A Tale from Camelot

HANNAH ATHOL

RESOURCE *Publications* · Eugene, Oregon

THE LADY OF THE FOUNTAIN
A Tale from Camelot

Resource Publications
An Imprint of Wipf and Stock Publishers
199 W. 8th Ave., Suite 3
Eugene, OR 97401

www.wipfandstock.com

PAPERBACK ISBN: 979-8-3852-5588-7
HARDCOVER ISBN: 979-8-3852-6408-7
EBOOK ISBN: 979-8-3852-6409-4

To Teri and Dan

Contents

Preface

SCIENCE IS MY TRADE, but one must have something in between experimenting and thesis writing. In this poem, I retell my favorite story from Camelot, first told by French poet Chrétien de Troyes in the 12th century. There is something dreamlike about those old tales. I have tried to tell my story with a little more organization, at the very least with an arch of a beginning, middle, and end. Yet I hope that Medieval dreamlike quality still shines through. What motivates these people? Why do they value the things they do? Why must one run off into the woods, pour water on a rock, and fight the knight who appears?

I would like to thank my family, and have dedicated this work to my parents, who chose to homeschool me so that I could follow any fanciful topic that took my interest, whether it was something useful like bioengineering or something niche, like Camelot. I would also like to thank my grandmother, a librarian, a lifelong lover of books; my brother, for all our childhood adventuring; my great-grandmother, teller of stories; my friends, especially those who have shared in my enthusiasm for writing; my teachers, especially those who introduced me to these tales and showed me more of the Medieval mind. Most of all, I thank my husband, who was charmed by my early attempts to impress him by telling him about the ridiculous chivalric adventures I'd been reading that week.

1

THE FOUNTAIN

"Listen, my friends," said Sir Calogrenant,
"It's darkness, that forest, a horrible haunt."
Sir Kay unsuccessfully stifled a laugh
At this tale of a fountain that quivered and quaffed.
Though further they prodded, he would not shed light
Why early that morning, this most hapless knight
Had entered the halls without horse gently trotting,
Sans hauberk, sans helmet, feet unshod and throbbing.
The three walked in combat of wittiest words,
The shamed knight, the haughty Sir Kay, and a third,
The courtly Yvain, whose more good-humored jest
All knew kept him merry on arduous quest.

A listening lady o'erheard them who fought
A lady - that Lady - of all Camelot,
Her beauty unmatched in all courts of the kings,
Her praise highest prize in the tournament's ring.
She gathered her gowns, all embroidered with gold,
With fine fairy fingers clutched colorful fold
Of fabric rinsed warm under prism of green,
Red, violet, and blue from Madonna's glass gleam.
She passed through the door and the knights gave their due,
Then she asked to know all of Calogrenant's rue.
For a Queen's still a lady; when intrigue is piqued
She'll rest not 'til sated with answers she seeks.

"Good knight," she requested, "Do hold nothing back.
Your shame is, though proper, but excess of tact.
For you know that my husband keeps only the best
Round his table; but I must know all of the quests."
"Alas, my fair Queen," said Sir Calogrenant,
"You know I must tell it, although I wish not.
I quested a wood so peculiarly dark
That when I perceived a singular lark
Enshrined, as it seemed, on a singular beam –
Sunlight breaking through the most ghastly of trees –
Where it sat, on a stone, that the blackest of all,
I crept to see closer, and that was my fall.

"For around that black stone flowed a stream of black ink
(Or it seemed, for the oaks shrouded all to the brink),
And beside it, a bowl. Could any knight ask
A clearer instruction for this questly task?
I ladled the water, I poured on the stone,
Behold! All the darkness about me was gone.
For the trees creaked aside, and the good sun shone through
And around me the songbirds sung sweetly and flew,
The hart and the hare came serenely, stood fast
As though I had entered at Eden at last,
But though this would coax me into dream-like phase
A storm swept upon us with Hadean craze.

"All the oaks swayed 'til I thought they would crack,
The lightning clawed o'er us with thunder a-thwack,
In vain I tried shielding my steed from the hail
As I prayed God to pity us fair creatures frail.
As sudden this started, it came to a stop
And I wondered at sound of a heavy clip-clop:
Then a black knight, his black horse in a prance,
Solemnly charged us and raised up his lance.
I'd hardly a moment to brace in my seat
When he sent me a-flying a good seven feet,
Stole my armor, and led off my horse at a trot
And so I came helpless back to Camelot."

Indignant, Yvain replied, shaking his fist,
"Good cousin, at once I'll avenge you of this.
By duty of kin, regain honor that's yours.
I'll send his head rolling; I did at the Tours!
No cousin of mine, no knight of the King
Should have to endure such ignominy.
I'll find this dark forest, and pour on that stone,
And when he appears, I will face him alone.
I'll not let appearance of Eden distract,
And when storm appears, I'll hold temper in tact.
Then when he is vanquished, I'll force him to swear
Allegiance to Arthur, and all in his care."

2

THE QUEST

Yvain had his sword sharpened swift by the best
Then saddled his steed and strode out on his quest.
King Arthur approved, though determined to follow
With travelling court, to seek out that dark hollow.
For every brave heart wished to see such strange things:
A lone knight defending mysterious springs.
But Yvain led the troop, even rode out alone
That he might be first at the water and stone
For he wished to face the Black Knight at that fount
And avenge his own cousin, Sir Calogrenant.
As he trotted, the wood became murky and still
'Til single sound called him – that small lark's sweet trill.

He looked, and there stood he, sunbeamed on a stone,
He hopped, tilt his head, gave a chirp, and was gone.
Yvain found the fountain. He lifted the bowl,
He poured out the water, awaited the call.
The sunlight burst forth to triumphantly show
The beauty of oak trees, spring-clad and aglow,
The finches, like fairies, they fluttered and danced
And trusting, the does, with their fawns, by him pranced.
Wild boars, tame as troubadours, knelt at his side;
A bear through the stream passed with lumbering stride;
In spite of himself, the wise, noble Yvain
Found his heart gently swelling, his courage struck tame.

A quiver of earth, and Yvain was awake.
The animals fled while the ground gave a shake.
The darkness engulfed him, and comets flew by
All fiery, then fizzled while whistling by.
Yvain's horse had heeded at war's trumpet-call
But battery by nature he knew not at all.
He stamped and he snorted; the knight reigned his beast;
The thick, icy rain scared him not in the least.
He sat on his mount, ignored thunder and hail;
The steed felt his courage, took heart, flicked his tail.
Then all the storm settled to eerie thin light;
There, in the shade, loomed the lurking Black Knight.

They lifted their lances, full gallop they flew,
Wood shields splintered sharply, but lances held true.
Each raced for his sword to be first at the strike;
Metal clanged upon metal and echoed with spite.
Muscles strained as, 'neath armor, their skin bruised to blue,
While each horse stood stately as good horses do.
For every knight knows, when his rival he forces
Surrender, though he fail, one must never strike horses.
So each with rapidity, metal, and might
Attempted to unhorse the other great knight.
The swords never slowed in their deadly attack
'Til, Lo! Yvain's sword broke through helmet and cracked.

Stunned, the Black Knight wavered vaguely with dread,
He clutched at his helmet and saw that he bled.
In stupor he grasped 'til he got at his reigns,
Headed off in the forest - so followed Yvain.
They galloped, they leapt, in the heat of the chase
Yvain did not notice the blood on his face,
The sweat, nor the strain, nor the wounds from the fight
With dark but still clearly so skillful a knight.
And yet they both knew they must fight to the end;
One a fountain, the other his honor, defend.
Whether death or surrender that end, they knew not.
Then Yvain heard their horses on cobble roads clop.

6

3

THE RING

A castle appeared with a circling moat,
And towards it they charged with a panting approach;
The Black Knight, sore wounded, fled fast for his life,
Alerted tower guards at their post with his cries.
Even now Yvain saw the great portcullis lowered
As his foe ran ahead, and beneath it maneuvered.
In only a moment he might make it past,
Finish fight in the city; it fell far too fast.
Yvain reached the first, and it just missed his back
Alas! For his noble horse, all sinews snapped.
The portcullis sliced the great stallion in half -
He perished as he lived: fierce, focused, steadfast.

Before looking up, Yvain heard the next gate
Close crashing; the Black Knight had made his escape.
At once Yvain found himself trapped at both sides,
Beneath arched stone hall, with no corner to hide.
He slipped into shadow where through bars he peered:
The townsfolk now saw their Black Knight and took fear.
His wounds would soon kill him; they knew it the truth
When they lifted him off his horse in a swoon.
They vanished; he waited; in wails, they returned
In black silken robes, their dead hero they mourned.
Night fell as the funeral procession ensued
And they carried their knight to his stony white tomb.

Last in the march was a lady in veil,
The lantern fire flickered her face as she wailed.
Yet no tears could mask undeniable truth:
This lady had fairness beyond all he knew.
A black veil framed a face porcelain, fine -
As only a virtuous life can enshrine
Into cheek angel-sculpted, lips rose with soft blush,
Fingers that softly yet earnestly clutched,
Eyelashes enmeshed those clear eyes with such grace
That no swelling tears could their virtues erase.
Despair pierced his heart as Yvain realized
He most, of all men, she must wholly despise.

This grief gripped his thoughts; he knew not when at last
The finalmost rites of the burial were past.
Love swift pierced his heart; but the townspeople turned
From grief to revenge; now for bloodlust they burned.
Firm his Love fixed him; Yvain's fate seemed set,
Then happened upon him fair damsel Lunete.
This damsel was one of that fine Lady's court,
It was not her custom with crowds to consort;
When all else were shaking at scandal or woe,
She knew how to keep her good Lady enthroned.
When she found this strange knight between portcullis hiding
She guessed who he was but sought first his own tiding.

"Circumstances betray you, Sir Knight," said Lunete.
Yvain started, then bowed at this damsel he met.
"Lady, please know that this knight of your city
Disgraced my own people; I slew him by duty."
Slowly she stepped through the shadow to see
How mighty and courtly this knight seemed to be.
"They seek you; they'll hear not your case, Sir," she hissed
As the mob's shouts rose up with the dawn's early mist.
"You can see that in here you have no place to hide;
You can prove your word later, but first, follow mine.
I've here" - now she pulled off a small ruby ring
Set in gold and entwined with old Celt engraving -

8

"A token, a test of your chivalrous merit;
When one pure of heart yet endangered shall wear it
It encloaks one in - ether, shall we say. None will see you.
But beware, lest sin of hate or lies betray you."
"Damsel, I am true," said Yvain, "May God vindicate!"
So he put on the ring when the mob rushed the gate.
They opened the portcullis, entered all grim,
They swarmed set to murder their Lord's assassin.
"Look, his horse lies here, slain and in two.
These bars are of iron - how could he get through?"
Invisible, Yvain stood in silence and waited;
Though clanging with anger, they could not be sated.

They left the gate open in all their confusion;
He entered the city in peace, not intrusion.
He stepped to the damsel, and knelt at her feet
And promised a boon, as then it was meet.
"Nay, by your chivalry you've been proven true;
Thus for you, good Knight, there is yet more I can do."
Yvain bowed his head, for he saw that veiled face
Appearing in window lit yonder; she traced
His fallen gaze back to its source. "I perceive
You're captured by graces of Lady Laudine!
Fear not, for now, in the kingdom of Barenton
We lack Lord to save us our forest or fountain!"

4

LAUDINE

Lunete entered chambers all hung up in black.
Loud Laudine wailed; her damsel held back.
A dark veil draped over joyous stained glass,
Discoloring vibrancy normally passed.
So Lunete found her Lady, face hid in fold arms,
Esconced in her misery, despising her charms.
"My Lady," she said, "Do you not see how strange
Your despair? Of yourself, you've a spectacle made.
Time for mourning has past and your fountain lies desolate;
You've forgotten your late Lord's love lacked, and his reprobate
Manner and character; surely his vice
Equipped him to so long that duty suffice!"

"Begone, wicked girl!" So Lunete sought Yvain
To continue at playing her sly, courtly game.
She tended her knight who'd been secretly hid
And asked him what sort of a day he had lived.
"Pleasantly spent," he sighed. "Forsooth, for shame!
Pleasant indeed! Are you ill or insane?"
But Yvain did not mind at this prison-like hiding
For a lover's a prisoner of sorts, soft and sighing.
So Lunete and Laudine kept their bickering. "What good
Is all this excess?" "I'd join him, if I could."
"God forbid!" cried Lunete, and insisted the might
Of their God could bring forth a more lordly a knight.

Laudine dismissed Providence, foolish indeed,
But Lunete moved her feint to a practical need.
For Barenton had heard that King Arthur and court
Sought after her fountain, and who would purport
To defend it? "You know that your servants are knaves,
Neither firm with their fists nor in battles are brave.
No, you need a husband! This kingdom, a King,
Defending your people, yourself, and your spring.
You refuse to acknowledge that any could do it,
But a better can serve, if accepted - I'll prove it."
"What nonsense. Name him to me; I will refute!"
"Nay, you'll not take good sense, but instead you'll rebuke!"

"I promise my temper withheld," swore Laudine.
Cautious, Lunete made her point: "Does it seem
When knights clash in battle, it's unclear who's better?
The pursued or pursuer? The vanquished or victor?
No, the knight who defeats in fair fight proves his case
As all who have wisdom will rightly embrace."
Laudine broke her oath and irately dismissed
Her nonsensical, impudent damsel - "Yet this,"
She thought to herself, "He slew not in spite.
Would my lord not have killed him if had been his right?
Aggrieved I may be, but of hate, there's no cause
For this strange knight has only but kept the land's laws."

A week more of this, and Lunete heard her Lady
Subtly inquire for Yvain, even lauding
The skill and the courage of him she knew not;
Lunete of his worth would hints secretly drop;
The court pressed their Lady take husband again,
Fulfill duties of lineage, throne, and fountain -
Yet none they suggested would dare mount a steed
To save his own life, much less rise at the need.
The maid could then hint that she'd identified
Their Secret Knight, claiming that she had sent spies.
Laudine could not hide all her eager interest,

Her desire to know this man, modest, victorious.

"His name is Yvain," said Lunete, "Son of Urien."
"A son of a King! . . . A match could be appropriate."
Meanwhile Lunete had her hidden knight tended,
Washed and clothed richly, his wounds all well mended.
When she presented Yvain to Laudine
The two were in love with each other; one seen
From afar and with longing, the other, in dreams
Fulfilled, nay, surpassed, as he strolled through the beams
Of sunlight that warmed castle windows. He stepped
To the edge of her throne, lift her fingers; he kept
His eyes upon hers as he stooped low to kiss
Her fingers, and soon their vows bid them to bliss.

5

THE TOURNAMENT

Deep in the forests of Broceliande,
King Arthur advanced with Sir Calogrenant,
Kay, Erec, Gareth, Gawain, and Sir Lancelot,
Percival, Pelleas - in short, all of Camelot.
The knights were accompanied by footmen and squires,
Their archers and lackeys, cooks, pages, and friars,
On palfreys and rounceys or else all on foot,
A desolate fountain they sought as a troop.
Now they took their time, for they drank and were merry,
Were pleased to, in every town, mingle and tarry,
But at last in the wilderness found it the same.
Sir Kay lost no time: "Now where is Yvain?"

He trotted his horse back and forth as he taunted:
"How he swore to avenge his good cousin, he vaunted
As only fools do; nay, only a coward
Would boast as he did, for a hero is dour
If he hears any praise of his virtue or prowess.
But a coward? He alone will his merits profess!
I can only approve of all his vapid boasting -
For who else would praise him, with trumpets and toasting?"
"Peace, peace," said Gawain, "And let the King pour.
He is not here to answer; we wish to explore."
"Aye," said Sir Kay, "But it please my King, grant,
When the Black Knight comes, I be the one to him lance."

This the King granted, then with great ceremony,
He spilled out the water, and all of the cacophony
Unfurled, as this tale has already related;
Yvain appeared once this chaos had abated.
Now Yvain was full suited in black; coat-of-arms
He ne'er donned when defending his good Lady's charms.
Thus, they knew him not. Now Sir Kay held his lance,
'Neath his armor, he smirked, and at him advanced.
They charged, and Yvain struck a well-aimed assault
Sending Kay off his horse in a full somersault.
He trotted his beast to King Arthur, agape,
And said, "Thus to all who dare tamper this lake."

All hailed at his voice, giving Sir Kay the grace
To come to himself, straight his sword, and save face.
The party continued at Barenton's hall
With banquet and hearing Yvain tell it all -
His adventure, his battle, his magical ring,
His capture by love, his beloved Laudine.
Now when this named Lady arrived at the feast,
They cheerily toasted her fountain's increase;
Festivities followed with dancing, good ale,
Music and laughter and troubadour tales.
For when brothers long parted unite, they'll for days
Rejoice in the heartiest, merriest ways.

"Come," said Gawain, while the roast pig they ate,
"When wed, to their shame, men too oft degenerate.
You must join our tournament, soon in our Camelot;
You've duties, but surely you'll cast in your lot?
You must fight in all of the training and games,
And when that is through, return swift to your dame."
Yvain could not bear to be long from his love,
But all knights seek constant their valor to prove.
He decided to seek of his wife a few days;
A fortnight, perhaps; he'd not long be away.
Laudine felt this deeply, but even she knew

Adventures are needed to keep the knights true.

She wavered. Then asked him: "Dear Husband, I wish
To ask but one thing." "Love, you know that I will."
"Depart for this tournament, joust with good cheer,
But linger no longer than one day and year.
To break this would forfeit my love and my vow,
Prove you faithless, though constant you would appear now."
Yvain said, "My Lady, you know all my heart.
I'll return e'en before the game's trumpet starts!"
When Camelot left through the Broceliande
Yvain joined them knowing his heart stayed behind.
In jousts and in feasts he spent many a day;
He triumphed and vanquished, proved merit at play.

Swift the time passed among fencings and joustings -
His Lady in solitude waiting and hoping -
One banquet preceded last glorious fight -
Then Yvain knew his oath, and he paled at the thought.
He started in anguish, but ere he could utter
A sound, in came one in a flurry and flutter.
She lighted her horse without gentleman's hand
Knelt for King and for Queen; held a small jeweled band.
"My Lady brings tidings of peace and of joy
To Arthur and Guinevere, and their employ,
Excepting Yain, that deceitful, false knight!"
Tossing ring, she snatched his; he stood speechless and white.

6

THE LION

Two ladies rode horseback among oaks at dawn:
A maid and her Lady, of great Noroisin.
White shimmering steeds they rode, though darkly clad;
They plotted protection for all of their land.
Beyond distant bramble, they gasped to behold
A man – unshorn, sleeping, completely unclothed.
Up they crept, quiet; concerned, they would try
To find some scratch by which they'd identify.
At his brow, the maid knew him who Camelot sought:
"At his Lady's rebuff, he fled where they knew not.
A more virtuous knight ne'er drew sword from its sheath;
Let not this sight sway you; 'tis madness from grief."

Knightly or no, he was unsound of mind,
So the Lady and maid sought of Morgan the Wise
An earthy good ointment they rubbed on his temples,
Set clothes at his side and slipped off, near and nimble.
Swift the cream worked on his tumors and brain:
He awoke and found much to his shock and his shame.
He hurriedly dressed, looking round in his fright,
Then saw the two maids drift like moons in twilight.
He called to them weakly; they saw him not first –
So they feigned, to his honor, being wise and courteous –
At long last they found him and leant their third steed,
So Yvain regained wits and strength by their good deeds.

Not long after lodging their castle that night,
Yvain found out all that had caused them their plight.
For a wicked Count plundered them then, and set fire
To their kingdom, waged war with each Sir and each Squire.
His heart rose in anger; Yvain drew his sword
And there slew those bandits; blood spilled to a pour,
'Til he last faced the Count. This relentless ferocity
So shocked him it stopped all his reckless animosity,
That he quaked at the tip of that dripping red sword,
So swore fealty, nay, slavehood, to her he'd abhorred.
Thus sworn, Yvain left, but they cried, "Sir, give name
By which we might praise you!" He turned by, ashamed.

The Lady and damsel knew why he was mute:
By broken word shamed, that they could not refute.
So sadly they told him they'd refrain to boast.
(Word slipped, I confess, and came known far, by most.)
But for now Yvain left them, to wander alone
To seek how he might for his Lady atone.
In sorrow he rode through a dark, gruesome wood,
When he heard a great wail that sent chills through his blood:
There wrapped by scaled Serpent, roared proud and defiant,
Though near death in battle, a fine and fierce Lion.
That Serpent could only by poisoning vanquish,
Thus by false flame might it this fine beast extinguish.

Both serpent or lion could kill man, if hated,
But Yvain's pity went to the nobly created.
Wicked that dragon to cheat by false flames -
This crafty worm now faced the wrath of Yvain.
He drew his sword, striking those thick armored scales,
Thus it turned and spit fire and lashed with its tail.
In vain it hissed, biteless; Hell's hate will not do
When evil eyes seek spotless heart to subdue.
At long last he pierced it, sliced head off with spite;
Breathless he turned to the lion - would it fight?
No, the Lion bowed stately, he eased all his qualms,
Rested muzzle within the knight's sore, open palm.

New friends, they adventured - the Lion and Knight.
Their hunting was merry; matchless they could fight.
At dusk they approached a town where folk protested:
"You are welcome, Sir Knight, but lions are detested."
"Naught to fear," Yvain cried, "You must welcome us both!"
Reluctant they welcomed, then marveled its truth.
Their King was impressed with this knight's perfect courtesy;
Yvain enjoyed blessings of their hospitality,
But soon he observed sorrow piercing each soul.
When pressed, they confessed of one sadly betrothed.
"My sons are all stolen by Harpin of the Mountain -
That ogre! If he weds not my daughter, he'll slay them."

Yvain knew his duty; they dared not, nor need ask.
He spent one sleepless night and that morning took Mass.
He knelt in stone pews rinsed red by St. Jerome,
Confessed, made his prayers, and stepped into the cold.
Clouds of breath could be seen as he marched to his horse,
His Lion stretched claws, then was ready for force.
They watched from the battlements. Gray masked the sun
As the town all awaited this Giant, Harpin.
Noon marked the hour of that sloth beast's approach
Prodding six hapless youths he with spear oft reproached.
Unwavering in courage, Yvain watched and stood fast -
"Let down the drawbridge!" he cried. "Let me pass!"

Full speed Yvain charged at this grisly, smug brute;
Bear-skin blocked his lance, and he broke it in two.
With back-handed blow he knocked knight to the ground -
Before he could crush him, the Lion quick pounced.
The Giant was strong, but unarmed, for he trusted
Much in his might and the great size he boasted -
More unfeeling brute Yvain never had faced,
But he and the Lion that slow fist outpaced.
When at last this glum giant lie felled at their feet,
The city folk shouted with joy its defeat.
"Your name, Sir, that ever your fame we'll enlighten!"
"Name me not; call me only the Knight with the Lion."

7

LUNETE

In wonderful wanderings quested our knight,
Constant in virtue and peerless in fight.
The Lion, good-hearted, sat stone-like at duels;
His eyes watched, all hawk-like, for traitors and fools.
If one dared depart from all chivalrous laws,
The Lion would threaten a crush from his jaws.
So even the wickedest foes honest fought
With Yvain as he damsel's security sought.
For in seeking regain of good will of his Lady,
Yvain shared not name at each grateful entreaty,
But instead trusted word spread coast and countryside
As Defender of Women, the Knight with the Lion.

Alas! Who found he in village, while seeking
A room to warm rest him with bread, ale, sleeping:
Fair Laudine, all blue-veiled, yet fiery eyed
Against senseless mob, who with scorn cast aside.
Enraged, our fine Knight drew his sword - at his stature
Their rioting quieted a moment; encaptured
He found, at its center, the damsel Lunete.
"Sir Knight!" - her wrists bound - "Be my champion, I beg!
I'm of treason accused." Here mobs roared; Laudine groaned;
"And no knight takes my case, to with sword prove alone
My innocence. Three witnesses false fan the flames -
Have mercy, I pray, lest I burn at the stake."

"Woman chary of truth but abundant in lies!"
Yelled the mob, but Yvain would not heed all their cries.
He lifted his eyes and he saw three false knights,
Arrogant accusers, armed, able to fight.
Shocked to see stranger prepare for the battle,
They mocked, "Three-to-one; you'll be slaughtered as cattle!"
"Nevertheless, I shall take this pure damsel's true case;
Shall one die without trial? Let good Christ weigh the weights!"
They set down their torches and suited in armor -
Yvain held his Lion back, grumbling in anger -
The mob, at first eager to fan up the fire,
Now eager awaited this curious trial.

Now, Lunete did not know who had taken her cause,
But Laudine and her ladies knelt prayerful to God
That this knight would defend her, prove valiant, true,
So proving Lunete had been falsely accused.
Dismounting, he unsheathed his sword; he slow spun
His thin blade thrice, each time reflecting the sun.
Reviewing his fortunes by shrewd scan of faces
(The three subtle side-eyed), he guessed their bad graces.
He was first to the fight, fiercely lunged at the foremost
And quickly he clicked off their clumsy ripostes.
For three though they were, they were angry, not able;
His skill passed their sum; he was one of the Table.

But brothers-in-arms were these crafty fools;
They plotted to plunder by plying the rules.
Two vied with Yvain to evade vicious whacks
While the third snuck behind to strike blows at his back.
The Lion thus sprang to his feet with a roar
As he watched his knight shamefully stricken once more.
Still Yvain yelled command to sit out this affair;
One blow of his own had more brawn than all theirs.
Yet shocking and sly, they caught him unaware,
While weaponless women assisted with prayers.
When last sneak attack slumped him flat on the lawn,
The Lion leapt in, tearing hauberk like straw.

His white teeth worked deftly: he ripped out entrails
And gnawed them, blood smearing; the brothers turned pale.
Forgetting the trial, the two turned to slay
The perilous cat who had turned them to prey.
When Yvain lift his head, instinct clearing wound's fog,
And was wroth, for they kicked at his beast like a dog.
So each brimming wrath for the other's dear sake,
They vanquished those wicked conspirers of hate.
Thus done, Yvain bound them to that spired stake
They'd prepared for Lunete, for grim justice's sake,
Saying, "He who false judges a man with his breath
Should suffer at once the same manner of death."

Now Lady Laudine her good damsel embraced,
Her accusers aflame in their abject disgrace.
The Knight and the Lion claimed wounds passing sore,
But they readied to march, so Laudine soft implored:
"I beg you to stay, and your Lion as well,
Let my leeches attend you, restore your good health!"
Though she, more than wounds, struck his heart with her pleas,
'Til his Lady's good favor restored, he'd not tarry.
Laudine was surprised that so noble a knight
Had a lady so loveless, yet seeing him quite
Unmoving, she answered, "May God give you joy
Where now you have sorrow!" And Lunete knew his ploy.

'Neath his helmet, he harkened: "May God hear your prayer!"
Yet with such battle-blows he nor Lion long fared.
But Lunete secret sought them while slow on their quest
(And swore to keep secret, at Yvain's firm behest),
She told him of castle with sisters who'd mastered
All healing arts in their gardens and cloisters.
They said their adieus, then Yvain made last plea:
"I beg you, fair damsel, keep her heart towards me."
"My lord, you have nothing to fear, she is yours.
She knows you are matchless; none else she adores."
So Yvain carried on, in that castle he rested,
Among those good maidens their lives he entrusted.

8

THE DAUGHTERS OF NOIRE

In the Kingdom of Noire dwelt a lord and his daughters,
Each warbling as willows, alluring as water.
Rothwyn was the eldest – tall and auburn-haired,
Then Rowena, gold framing her face, fine and fair.
When their lord went to God, with no son of his own,
He trusted these two to lay claim, each her own.
But Rothwyn seized all, and she shameless turned out
Her own sister, ere mourning dare drift into doubt.
Being brazen, she plotted to best her by battle,
Lest Rowena with champion her seizure could rattle;
She gained good Gawain, lying greatly with gumption,
To secure best knight known, at that time, in her function.

Restless Rowena rode to Camelot,
Announced all her woes and demanded Lancelot.
Sir Yvain being lost, if Gawain was to fight
She was luckless unless that most legend'ry knight,
Sir Lancelot himself, could take up her case,
With sword and with strength bring that Rothwyn disgrace.
"Is it true," cried King Arthur, "my nephew Gawain
Has agreed to take arms for a cause so condemned?"
"My Lord," said Gawain, "she deceived me; she wrought
Her lies to ensnare, yet my word, I turn not."
"Alas!" said the King, "that in such days you call!"
For then was Sir Lancelot by Grail enthralled.

The noblest, mightiest knight of the land
The only, indeed, who could force Gawain's hand,
Was off on a quest, and one sacred and right,
But gone, and Rowena left luckless in plight.
King Arthur took pity on this gentle lass,
In scarlet and ermine, her riding cloak clasped,
Face eager despite all the depth of her woes,
And he gave forty days to find her a hero.
After bowing, she lightly leapt up on her steed
Left to seek some new noteworthy knight with great speed.
She knew one last chance who might face great Gawain -
Nameless Knight of the Lion, Defender of Dames.

Rowena rode out, on that goal she was set;
And found friendship and counsel in the fair Lunete.
She who that great knight had deftly defended
Told her such stories spectacular, splendid,
He seemed God's care for noble-hearted in need
Against giants, and dragons, and goblinish greed.
Thus encouraged, Rowena set off for that castle
(E'en now, those healers felt harried and hassled
In tending the paws of a Lion who growled
At tenderest touch of an ointment or salve.)
Thus directed, Rowena continued her chase
Halting rarely for rest, for so urgent her haste.

Through vast rolling fields all feathered in gold,
Rowena sought fiercely for knight she'd been told,
Took succor at the town where a giant lay felled
(For the Knight of the Lion, they rang out church bells).
One cold gleaming dawn she saw out on the heather
A beast - nay, a Lion! Her heart all a-quiver,
She raced to the site; there the good Knight she met,
Bright-eyed and breathless, her horse all a-sweat.
Not stopping for air, she told all of her plight;
In pieces, he patiently found out her fright.
Concluding this speech, he replied in all ease,
"Sweet friend, I shall go whithersoever you please."

Fast hoofbeats battered the roads to the trial,
When the two came upon a most curious isle,
The Isle of Damsels; each lady they saw
Was ghastly of face, fingers calloused and raw.
Their round grey eyes mournfully watched as they passed,
Though tattered in rags, each a gold spindle clasped.
These women all wandered a cold, craggy cave
Where out came fine fabrics they wore not, but made.
All of this roused the Knight's most fearsomely ire,
And he reigned his horse towards that sad land's tallest spires;
Rowena spoke not, but meek followed, head bowed,
For she knew such a knight would by evil be roused.

Inside that cold tow'r was a cowardly king,
Alone, but well fed, weary court attending.
At once Yvain asked why abused were those dames;
He was shocked at the soulless resignation he faced.
This king alone looked at his drawn sword in fright,
And he whimpered, "I prithee, have mercy, good Knight!
I was, in my youth, so reckless and wanton
I was faced, one dark night, by a Hell-fire Demon
Demanding my soul I'd unwittingly paid
By all those sins silky and slippery made.
Trembling I pled for new chances, some time;
That demon's eyes reddened and red was his smile.

"Cold my blood flowed through my villainous veins
When his twin stepped from shadows, said, 'There is one way,
If you can produce thirty damsels this night,
You'll have one year added your miserable life.
Rest not, for each year we'll return for some more:
Thirty souls for your own, we'll each annum implore.'
Loud were the wails of mothers that night
As my kingdom was plundered, by my own charge, my right.
Their daughters thus taken, they're enslaved by those things:
To my shame, I've been locked in this bargaining of beings."
Grave, Yvain turned to that cave in the north:
"God guard me, restoring this kingdom its joy!"

29

Straight Yvain went to the mouth of the cave,
And out came the creatures that kept all those slaves.
Yvain was aghast at their burls and bark,
Their knobby hands gnarled and branching in parts,
Rough twisted wood tangled up on their heads,
Yet limber and lithe and inspiring dread.
The Lion stood trembling, frozen in fear,
At the sight of these demons, two towering trees,
They, leafless and dead, each a cherry tree grasped
And brandished as swords, fencing fiercely and fast.
At each blow, Yvain strained all his nerves, strong and tense;
They broke shield and helmet, his dearest defense.

Excellent swordsmen he found them to be,
For they fought off his sword with their lightly held trees.
Fiercely Yvain threw the fight all his strength,
But they slowed not nor wearied as battle gained length.
Sweating and straining Yvain lost his sword,
And the Lion awoke from his fear with a roar.
Leaping upon the wood arm with a growl,
He snatched that tree-demon, dragged it to the ground.
Yvain took his chance: he retook his sharp steel,
And he found that wood devil upon the ground still.
Panic had entered red eyes of the first,
So Yvain and the Lion knew they could break the curse.

Deftly they worked to fell that second tree -
Each yelled hellish screams, but did so futilely.
Then Yvain took his sword and he sawed off their heads,
And at once that land's gloom was released from its dread.
The maidens came dancing, triumphant in song,
They lift fine red silks by which they had been wronged,
Embroidering gold when their rags clothed them poor,
And they waved them as flags waved triumphant in war.
The Isle of Damsels at peace once again,
Families mended, their King cut from sin -
They sent them with blessings, and music, and flowers,
The trio left trotting 'neath blossoming bowers.

9

THE TRIAL

Gold the sun glistened o'er ladies and knights,
Red and green tents for mingling and watching the fights.
All Camelot whispered this upcoming game,
Two Knights representing two quarrelling dames.
Rothwyn sat haughty, clad comely in green,
She'd given Gawain coat-of-arms in this vein,
Green banner on helmet, green griffon on shield,
To make him the hero of Noire in this deal.
Rowena, more simply adorned, sat in honor,
By Guinevere, favored by her and by Arthur.
When her hero emerged, the crowds murmured and muttered -
So this was the Knight who with Lion had wandered!

The Lion was courtly, strolled to the King's side,
And sat, as invited, paws precise, and with pride.
Whiskers spread wisely, half-shut in his eyes,
He would silently, solemnly survey and spy.
So Gawain and Yvain, though each bound like a brother,
Clad in arms clandestine, cast blows brash on each other.
They jousted and fenced, they breathlessly battled,
Nicked swords and hit shields all splintered and splattered,
Clanging echoes rang expertly, strong steel spun,
The crowd's gasps grew weary as the hour went long.
Their armor all dented, their brains beaten in -
How could each bear and blow with such might against him?

The Green Griffon thwacked; Red Lion rebuffed;
The Lion struck back, but the Griffon quick ducked.
A strike on a helmet repaid on the shins,
Their swords were nigh dancing with surely sent spins.
The Griffon misstepped – or, had he retreated?
Yet at that same moment, the Lion left heaving -
Each held up his hand while in vain, breath he caught,
Then each yelled, and even more ferociously fought.
The people began to glance up at their lord -
These knights were so perfectly matched, they were bored.
"Truly we've never seen knights so courageous!
Surely sisters can stoop, reconcile in good graces?"

At this, Rothwyn cried, "I shall not relent!"
In pity, Rowena looked rueful; the Queen lent
Her aid in addressing her husband: "Can you not
By right of a king, make this girl give her lot?"
But Arthur was irked by Rothwyn's lack of virtue:
"Why force half, when she might lose it all, and pride too?
No, I'll let these two at it: there's yet chance she'll fall,
And then her high manners will meet their downfall."
The Knights heard this banter; they regretted their King
Did not end that fight now, with all its misery,
They were winded and wearied, but determined to show
More gusto and glory than began all their blows.

"Good Knight, you are matchless," gasped out Sir Yvain,
He clang his sword constant: "Who are you?" "Gawain."
Yvain dropped his sword. "Ah, what mischance is this!
I'd surrendered at once if I'd known first of this!"
"Why, what is your name?" asked bewildered Gawain
(Though relieved to, this moment, from fighting refrain).
He removed his stained helmet and all knew the truth:
So Yvain was the Knight with the Lion, forsooth!
Gawain was aghast to behold his bruised friend,
Then collapsed at his knees to with Arthur contend.
"My King, at that moment, I knew I had failed,

I meant to resign; I am no longer able."

"No, my Lord!" cried Yvain, kneeling, "it cannot be -
It was I on the verge of surrender, not he!"
Thus the two each contended the other's great strength,
While claiming his own had run out at this length.
The King silenced both. He cried, "Where is that damsel
Who forcibly, cruelly, disinherited her sister?"
"Here I am!" she stepped forward - "Ah, so you confess!"
"Alas, you have trapped me!" "That ends that, nonetheless.
By your own word you've sinned; Lady Rowena, Noire is yours.
Now tend these bludgeoned battlers. Where stand my doctors?"
All but Rothwyn rejoiced that justice had been served,
As those knights praised the other victorious first.

10

THE END

Alone, enthroned, wrapped in velvets all blue,
Laudine lived and reigned with much sighing and rue.
Cerulean shards lit her throne from above
Enlightening a heart lingering loyal in love.
A thousand "if-only's" a-flit in her mind,
Blaming both, though her own became clearer with time.
When she heard of his madness, her court named him dead;
But this she refused, though it filled her with dread.
At first, she mused, "Pity his love so swift died,"
But at once knew this only to be a cruel lie.
"In truth, I have killed him - my pride both our foes -
Him slaying at once, I die daily and slow."

Thus Barenton she ruled, steeped in sorrows, but fair,
While her husband recovered in Camelot's care.
When Yvain first returned to his senses, he knew
It'd be not long until she heard all of his ruse.
Sick of love, he knew he must decisively act:
He'd insist that she meet him and break her ill pact.
If only her face he'd implore and address,
He'd convince her of all of his love, and confess,
He'd show how his blame he fought hard to atone,
Woo her back with his winnings, with Lion alone.
"Yes, this is my chance - her heart's soft yet, I know,"
He called to his Lion - "To the Fountain we go!"

To that forest they went: and then doubt plagued his brain.
What if she felt still bitter, bereaved, and betrayed?
Such a breaking of oath was a knight's greatest sin -
Surely she'd deign not to meet, nor give in!
At the Fountain he stooped slow to lift up the bowl
(As the Lion watched, curious, at the water crisp, cold);
He wavered a moment; drop by drop, tipped it out:
That Lark signaled all of his friends to exult.
The glad sun shone forth, and the trees awoke jovial,
Then he said, "I'll *insist* that she come at my call."
Frantic he poured it again and again
And chaos ensued in the wind and the rain.

Songbirds sang sudden as if in trance,
Doe and fawn confused darted, 'neath hail they danced,
Boar and bear went galumphing with chattering jaws,
Embarrassed, the Lion hid his eyes 'neath his paws.
He poured, and in Barenton, walls began crumbling,
Courtiers clasped at themselves, in fear fumbling,
Exasperated, Laudine left to face this great woe -
"Though death may await, to that Fountain I'll go!
That Fount, curséd cause of my joys and my griefs,
That my Lord brave defended, abhorred in my fief.
Alas, day should come I must face it alone -
If only vain oath I repented, long ago."

Laudine wrapped her mantle about her and went
While Eden and Chaos kept clashed at the Fount,
She arrived, and all stopped - both birdsong and rain.
The man she saw then was her good Lord Yvain!
What's more, was that Lion - so this was the Knight
Who'd rescued all damsels from all of their plights,
Who'd fought for the weary, the ragged, the worn,
Crushed evil to win back his Lady adored.
They rushed to embrace, cried for pity and pardon,
Their marriage restored where it started - this Fountain,
With Lion and love they spent all of their days
Bringing Barenton justice and mercy and peace.

www.ingramcontent.com/pod-product-compliance
Lightning Source LLC
Chambersburg PA
CBHW060629030426

42337CB00018B/3268